ABORIGINAL BIOGRAPHIES

Political Leaders

KAITE GOLDSWORTHY

Weigl

Published by Weigl Educational Publishers Limited
6325 10th Street SE
Calgary, Alberta T2H 2Z9
Website: www.weigl.ca

Library and Archives Canada Cataloguing in Publication

Goldsworthy, Kaite
Political leaders / Kaite Goldsworthy.

(Canadian Aboriginal biographies)
Includes index.
ISBN 978-1-77071-453-3 (bound).—ISBN 978-1-77071-457-1 (pbk.)

1. Indian civic leaders—Canada—Biography—Juvenile literature. 2. Native leaders—Canada—Biography—Juvenile literature. 3. Indians of North America—Canada—Politics and governmen—Juvenile literature. 4. Native peoples—Canada—Politics and government— Juvenile literature. I. Title. II. Series: Canadian Aboriginal biographies

E89.G65 2012 j971.004'9700922 C2011-908193-8

Printed in the United States of America in North Mankato, Minnesota
1 2 3 4 5 6 7 8 9 0 16 15 14 13 12

082012
WEP250612

Senior Editor: Heather Kissock
Art Director: Terry Paulhus

We acknowledge the financial support of the Government of Canada through the Canada Book Fund for our publishing activities.

CONTENTS

Introduction

SHAWN A-IN-CHUT ATLEO

The political system in Canada is a **democracy**. In a democracy, people elect representatives to pass laws and make decisions for them. Voters elect leaders they believe will represent them and their communities in the best way. In an election for a seat in a legislature or other political office, the individual with the largest number of votes wins the election.

The **Aboriginal** Peoples of Canada belong to First Nations, Inuit, and **Métis** communities. Not until 1960 did all Aboriginal Peoples in Canada win the right to vote in **federal** elections. Aboriginal Peoples have a long history in the country's political system, however. They have made many valuable contributions to government and politics in Canada, and they have served as political leaders.

Political leaders are people who are experienced or involved in the art and science of politics. Many hold a political office. Most are members of a **political party**. Political leaders work in all levels of government, including municipal, provincial or territorial, and federal governments. They can also work in other types of political organizations.

Several Aboriginal Canadians have held federal offices or provincial or territorial offices. Cree lawmakers Elijah Harper and Romeo Saganash and Dene leader Ethel Blondin-Andrew have served as **members of Parliament (MPs)**. **Inuk** MP Leona Aglukkaq became a **Cabinet** member. Another Inuk, Paul Okalik, won election as the first **premier** of the territory of Nunavut. Others, such as Shawn A-in-chut Atleo from the Ahousaht First Nation, have served as leaders of Aboriginal organizations. All these political leaders have overcome obstacles to represent the people. They have worked to make Canada a better place to live for all its citizens.

LEONA AGLUKKAQ

ETHEL BLONDIN-ANDREW

ELIJAH HARPER

PAUL OKALIK

ROMEO SAGANASH

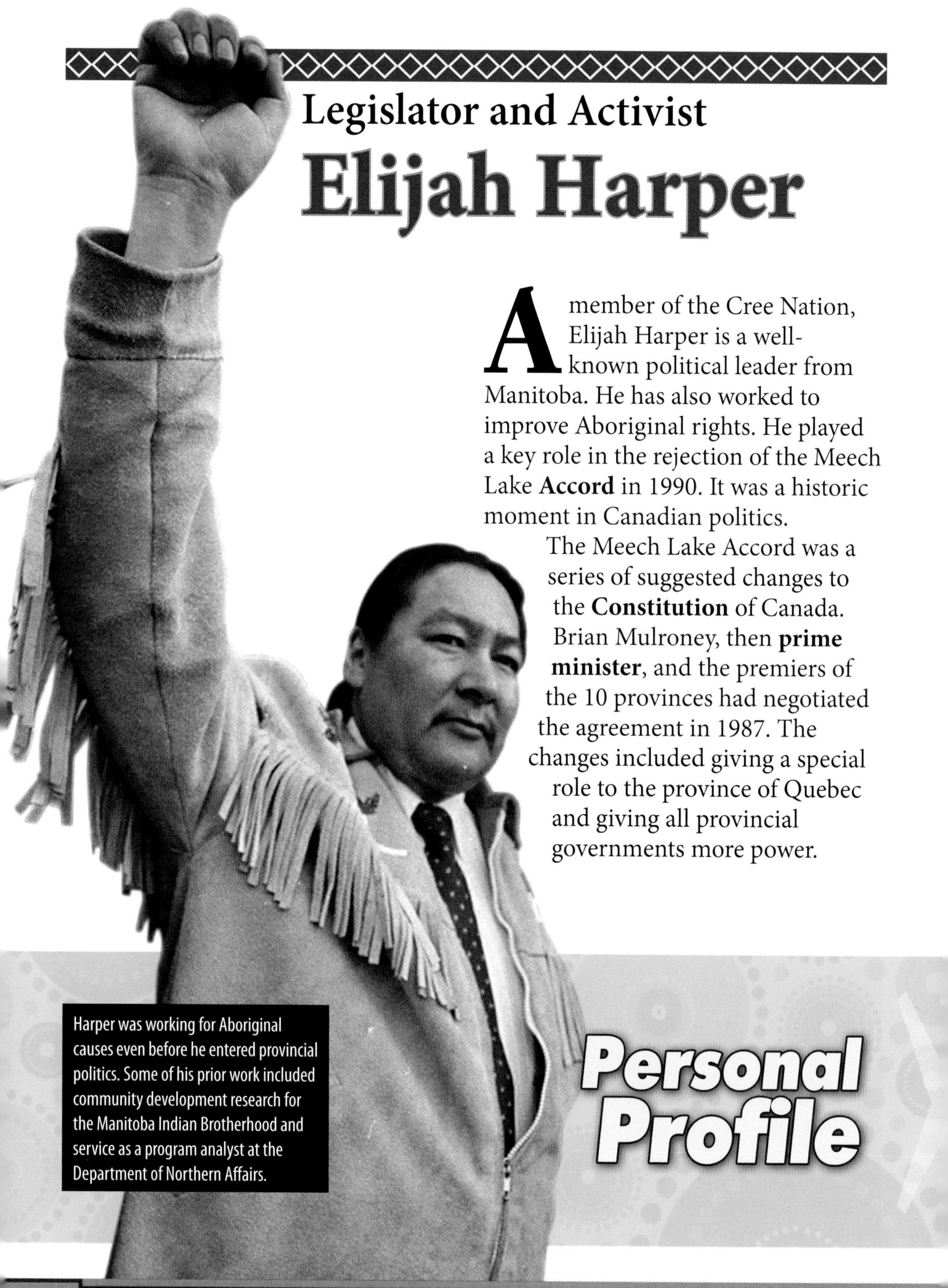

Legislator and Activist

Elijah Harper

A member of the Cree Nation, Elijah Harper is a well-known political leader from Manitoba. He has also worked to improve Aboriginal rights. He played a key role in the rejection of the Meech Lake **Accord** in 1990. It was a historic moment in Canadian politics.

The Meech Lake Accord was a series of suggested changes to the **Constitution** of Canada. Brian Mulroney, then **prime minister**, and the premiers of the 10 provinces had negotiated the agreement in 1987. The changes included giving a special role to the province of Quebec and giving all provincial governments more power.

Harper was working for Aboriginal causes even before he entered provincial politics. Some of his prior work included community development research for the Manitoba Indian Brotherhood and service as a program analyst at the Department of Northern Affairs.

Personal Profile

Many Canadians disagreed with the accord. Aboriginal groups, women's organizations, and other groups believed it did not address their concerns. In particular, many of the country's Aboriginal Peoples felt the accord ignored their role in the founding of Canada. They also felt that they had been excluded from the negotiations.

Official acceptance of the accord required the approval of all the provincial governments. The **Legislative Assembly** of Manitoba could not vote on the accord unless all members agreed to support introducing it for discussion. Elijah Harper, a member of the Legislative Assembly, refused to agree and allow a vote. He argued that the accord did not recognize the status and rights of the country's Aboriginal Peoples. After the Newfoundland and Labrador legislature refused to vote on it, too, the accord failed. One Cree lawmaker with a powerful message had blocked a major national constitutional change. It was a reminder of the importance of Aboriginal citizens in the country's political process.

"We're the First Nations people. We're the very people who welcomed [Prime Minister Brian Mulroney's] ancestors to this country, and he didn't want to recognize us in the Constitution."

Early Years

Elijah Harper, born in 1949, was raised on the Red Sucker Lake **reserve** in northern Manitoba. He spent his early years with his grandparents. Harper learned many Aboriginal traditions from his grandparents, including hunting, trapping, and the use of herbal medicine.

Harper was sent to a government-run **residential school** as a boy. There, he was forced to speak English and live without his traditions. Despite this challenge, his Aboriginal identity remained strong. His knowledge of the Cree culture and language did, too.

BORN Elijah Harper was born on March 3, 1949, on the Red Sucker Lake reserve in northern Manitoba to Allan and Ethel Harper. His father was a pastor. Harper was the second of 13 children.

FAMILY Harper married Elizabeth Ann Ross in 1972. He has both children and stepchildren.

EDUCATION Harper received his high school diploma in Winnipeg, Manitoba. In 1971, he studied for one year at the University of Manitoba.

CAREER Harper has served as a member of the Legislative Assembly of Manitoba, a provincial government **minister**, and an MP. He is also an honorary chief for life.

“I believe if we go back to our roots, principles, and beliefs, we can gain our direction.”

Developing Skills

After graduating from high school in Winnipeg, Harper studied anthropology at the University of Manitoba. He began working with the Manitoba Indian Brotherhood, a group that tried to improve Aboriginal rights, and with the Manitoba Department of Northern Affairs. When he was just 29 years old, Harper became chief of the Red Sucker Lake First Nation.

In 1981, Harper was elected to the Legislative Assembly of Manitoba for Rupertsland. It was the first time an Aboriginal lawmaker had ever served in Manitoba's legislature. In 1986, he was appointed to the provincial Cabinet. The following year, Harper was named the minister of Northern Affairs for Manitoba. He held that position until 1988.

Harper left the Legislative Assembly of Manitoba to run for federal office in 1992. It was a big step. Harper was elected to the **House of Commons** for the **riding** of Churchill. He served from 1993 to 1997.

The Path to Success

In 1995, Harper organized a gathering of thousands of people, called the Sacred Assembly, in Hull, Quebec. His goal was to encourage friendship and understanding among Canadians from all backgrounds and faiths.

As a result of the Sacred Assembly, June 21 was declared National Aboriginal Day. Now, people

On July 22, 1990, Harper led a group of about 1,000 Aboriginal people through Winnipeg, Manitoba, on a march to show their support for the Mohawk community in Quebec, Ontario. The Mohawks were in a dispute with the town of Oka over land rights.

across the country celebrate and recognize Canada's Aboriginal Peoples on this day.

Harper has always been passionate about human rights. He is an **advocate** for the rights of **indigenous peoples** around the world. In fact, in 1991, Harper received a human rights award from the Ontario Public Service Employees Union. South African leader Nelson Mandela received the same honour, called the Stanley Knowles Award, the previous year.

In 1999, Harper was appointed the commissioner of the Indian Claims Commission. This group was created in 1991 to settle disputes over land ownership between First Nations peoples and the government of Canada. He held the post for two years. Harper continues to be a strong advocate for equal rights for people in Canada and the rest of the world.

Accomplishments

1981 Harper is elected a member of the Legislative Assembly of Manitoba.

1986 Harper is appointed to the Cabinet of Manitoba.

1990 The Red Sucker Lake First Nation awards Harper the title of honorary chief for life. The governor general gives Harper a commemorative medal of Canada to honour his public service.

1993 Harper is elected to the House of Commons.

1995 Harper organizes the first Sacred Assembly in Hull, Quebec.

1996 Harper wins an achievement award for public service from the National Aboriginal Achievement Foundation, now called Indspire.

2008 *Elijah*, a film based on the story of Harper's life and shot entirely in Manitoba, is released.

Teacher and Lawmaker

Ethel Blondin-Andrew

A Dene from Canada's North, Ethel Blondin-Andrew achieved several firsts in Canadian politics. Her decision to run in the 1988 general election was historic. At that time, no Aboriginal women had ever been elected to the House of Commons. She campaigned and won her riding of Western Arctic, becoming the first Aboriginal woman elected to Parliament.

Blondin-Andrew ran for re-election in 1993. After she won, she was appointed secretary of state for Training and Youth and then for Children and Youth. Andrew-Blondin was appointed the minister of state for Children and Youth in 2003. That made her the country's first

Personal Profile

Blondin-Andrew was known throughout her political career as an advocate for Aboriginal people, children, and persons with disabilities. One of her key initiatives was including Aboriginal communities in workforce programs.

Aboriginal woman member of the Cabinet. The following year, she became the minister of state for Northern Development.

During Blondin-Andrew's time in government, she worked on youth employment and homelessness. Her efforts to improve the lives and health of Aboriginal women led to recognition from several groups. The Institute for the Advancement of Aboriginal Women, for example, admitted her into the Circle of Honour in 2004 for her leadership skills.

"This is about enabling and empowering the Aboriginal Peoples of Canada . . . to have a future in Canada like that of everyone else."

Early Years

Ethel Blondin-Andrew, born in 1951, grew up in the Sahtu Region of the Mackenzie Valley in the Northwest Territories. There were several children in her family. As a child, Blondin-Andrew learned to trap on muskrat and beaver hunts. Her grandparents and parents taught her to appreciate nature, respect the past, and speak the Dene-Slavey language.

In 1959, Blondin-Andrew was sent to Grollier Hall, a residential school in Inuvik in the MacKenzie Delta. She was required to speak English and to learn European-Canadian ways of life. Like many other Aboriginal Peoples in Canada, Blondin-Andrew calls herself a "survivor" of the residential schools.

Grollier Hall was a student residence run by the Roman Catholic Church. It first opened in 1959 for students from the Sahtu, Beaufort Delta, and Kitikmeot regions. Students who lived here attended the Inuvik Federal School.

BORN Ethel Dorothy Blondin-Andrew was born on March 25, 1951, in Fort Norman, now called Tulita, in the Northwest Territories.

FAMILY Ethel Blondin-Andrew is married to Leon Andrew. She is the mother of three children, Troy, Tanya, and Tim, from a previous marriage.

EDUCATION Blondin-Andrew received a bachelor of education degree from the University of Alberta in 1974.

CAREER Blondin-Andrew has worked as a teacher and an Aboriginal languages specialist. She has also served in the House of Commons and in the federal Cabinet.

"I am evidence of the fact that First Nations people can succeed, not because I was born rich or because I was privileged, but because I have worked hard and there have been opportunities given to me which I have taken."

Developing Skills

When she was 14 years old, Blondin-Andrew began attending the Grandin College Leadership Program in Fort Smith in the Northwest Territories. Unlike a residential school, this program offered Blondin-Andrew the opportunity to learn valuable leadership skills. Its goal was to teach discipline and develop future leaders.

Blondin-Andrew then earned a diploma from the Teacher Education Program at Arctic College. She decided to pursue her love of teaching. In 1974, she graduated from the University of Alberta with a bachelor of education degree. She was one of the first certified Aboriginal teachers to work in Canada's North. She also worked as an Aboriginal language specialist, teaching and helping to preserve Aboriginal language and culture. Teaching has remained a lifelong passion for her.

Blondin-Andrew's first experience with politics was in 1984 when she served as the national manager of indigenous training and development with the Public Service Commission of Canada in Ottawa, Ontario. After two years, she returned to the Northwest Territories. There, she worked for the territorial government in Yellowknife as an assistant deputy minister for culture and communications.

Blondin-Andrew served as a member of Paul Martin's Cabinet. She and other Cabinet members were sworn in at a ceremony in Ottawa on December 12, 2003.

The Path to Success

During her life, Blondin-Andrew has understood the obstacles facing the Aboriginal Peoples of Canada. She has always been a vocal supporter of the rights of Aboriginal citizens in the country. Women, children and teenagers, and people with physical and mental disabilities are her focus. Her work as an advocate has helped to raise awareness of the many issues facing Aboriginal youth, particularly in Canada's North. Blondin-Andrew has also worked to ensure that Aboriginal communities are included in government job programs throughout Canada.

In the 2006 election, Blondin-Andrew lost her seat in the House of Commons. After she left Parliament, she continued to inspire Canadians as a speaker and supporter of Aboriginal issues. Blondin-Andrew has also advised corporations with an interest in the natural resources of the Northwest Territories.

Accomplishments

1974 Blondin-Andrew graduates from the University of Alberta.

1988 Blondin-Andrew becomes the first Aboriginal woman elected to Canada's Parliament.

1993 She is appointed the secretary of state for Training and Youth.

2001 Brock University in Ontario gives Blondin-Andrew an honorary doctorate for her service to the Aboriginal Peoples of Canada.

2003 Blondin-Andrew becomes the minister of state for Children and Youth.

2004 She is appointed the minister of state for Northern Development.

2012 The Status of Women Council presents Blondin-Andrew with a Wise Women Award.

Lawyer, Politician, and Advocate

Romeo Saganash

Romeo Saganash is a lawyer and political leader. He is the first Cree in the history of Quebec to earn a law degree. In 2011, he was elected to serve in the House of Commons for the Abitibi–Baie-James–Nunavik–Eeyou riding in Quebec. It is the province's largest riding. It is also one of the largest ridings in Canada.

In the House of Commons, Saganash focusses on several areas. As a member of the Committee on Foreign Affairs and International Development, he

Saganash has been involved in politics and advocacy groups for much of his life. In addition to Aboriginal rights, his areas of expertise include regional development and the environment.

works on global issues. Saganash also serves as an associate member of the Committee on Aboriginal Affairs and Northern Development, as well as the Finance Committee.

Although Saganash is new to Parliament, he has been active in political issues for nearly 30 years. He has worked to protect the environment as chair of the James Bay Advisory Committee on the Environment. He also served as vice chair of the Cree Regional Authority, which is responsible for environmental protection in Cree communities. Helping Aboriginal businesses succeed without damaging the natural world is another priority for Saganash.

Early Years

Romeo Saganash was born in 1962. He was raised in Waswanipi, a small Cree community in Quebec. His family included 14 children.

Saganash was raised with Cree traditions. As a child, he watched his father making snowshoes and building a canoe. Saganash spent time hunting, fishing, and trapping with his brothers and sisters.

When Saganash was about seven, the Canadian government took him and four of his siblings from their home. They were placed in a residential school. Later, Saganash learned that his father had died. The school could not afford to send him and his siblings home for the funeral. Saganash says this was a turning point in his life, explaining that he decided to "move on from the rage [of being taken away], to try to take the best from a very bad condition and circumstance."

"I learned that, by virtue of our connection, we are interdependent, supporting and supported by each other. And I learned that our mutual reliance—our community—demands that we make the effort to understand and respect each other and the role each of us plays."

BORN Romeo Saganash was born on October 28, 1962, in Waswanipi, Quebec. He is one of 14 children.

FAMILY Saganash is the father of three grown children.

EDUCATION Saganash earned a law degree from the University of Quebec in Montreal.

CAREER Saganash has worked as a lawyer, a deputy grand chief, and an advocate for the environment.

Developing Skills

Saganash spent 10 difficult years in the Canadian residential school system. After this experience, he wanted Cree youth to feel involved in politics and decision making and proud of their heritage. He helped found the Cree Nation Youth Council in 1985. Saganash hoped to shape and guide future Aboriginal leaders by establishing this organization.

As part of the race for leadership of the New Democratic Party (NDP), Saganash participated in debates with the other candidates. These types of debates give candidates an opportunity to express their opinions about various issues.

"*Canada prospers when all of us live in dignity, when everyone understands and shares in equal and equitable treatment under the law.*"

Saganash graduated from the University of Quebec with a law degree in 1989. His education as a lawyer helped Saganash in his work with the Grand Council of the Crees. This is the governing body for the Cree people of Quebec. He served in this organization first as deputy grand chief and then as director of Quebec Relations and International Affairs.

In 2002, Saganash was one of the main authors of a $4.5 billion settlement for the James Bay Cree. The agreement, called *La Paix des Braves*, which is French for "The Peace of the Braves," settled many years of lawsuits against the Quebec government. Saganash also worked on the United Nations Declaration on the Rights of Indigenous Peoples in 2007. He is a respected authority on Aboriginal rights, the Constitution, international law, and human rights.

The Path to Success

In 2011, Saganash became the first Cree MP in the history of the province of Quebec. On September 16, 2011, he entered the race to lead the political party called the New Democratic Party (NDP) of Canada. In 2012, however, he announced that he was withdrawing from the leadership race. Saganash said that he needed more time to care for his mother, sisters and brothers, and children. He also noted that his chances of winning were hurt by a lack of financial support. Saganash is believed to be the first Aboriginal person to seek the leadership of a major Canadian political party.

Accomplishments

1985 Saganash helps to establish the Cree Nation Youth Council.

1989 Saganash earns a law degree.

1993 Saganash becomes deputy grand chief of the Grand Council of the Crees, an office that he holds until 1995.

1997 He begins serving as the chair of the James Bay Advisory Committee on the Environment.

2002 Saganash helps negotiate the historic *Paix des Braves* settlement between the James Bay Cree and the Quebec government.

2011 Saganash is elected to Parliament from the Abitibi–Baie-James–Nunavik–Eeyou riding.

Lawyer and Premier

Paul Okalik

A new Canadian territory was created in 1999 out of the eastern part of the Northwest Territories. This separate territory was named Nunavut. *Nunavut* means "our land" in Inuktitut. Inuktitut is a group of languages spoken by the Inuit of central and eastern Arctic Canada.

Canada's largest territory, Nunavut is home to more than 25,000 people. Many residents are Inuit. The territory of Nunavut has what is known as a consensus government. This means that members of the legislature are elected as individuals, rather than as members

Okalik entered politics because he believed it was the best way for him to help his fellow Inuit.

Personal Profile

of a political party. Once the individual members have been elected, they choose one legislator to be the territory's premier.

In the territory's first election, in 1999, Inuk lawyer Paul Okalik won a seat in the Nunavut Legislative Assembly, to represent the Iqaluit West riding. His fellow assembly members then chose him to become the first premier of Nunavut. He was sworn in on the same day, April 1, that Nunavut became an official Canadian territory. It was a historic day for Nunavut and a personal triumph for Okalik.

Early Years

Paul Okalik was born in 1964 in Pangnirtung, Nunavut, which was then

Pangnirtung is located on Baffin Island. It has a population of about 1,300.

"I'm living my dream, and I want every young person to have the same opportunity."

part of the Northwest Territories. He was the youngest of 10 children born to traditional Inuit hunter Auyaluk and his wife, Annie. The family lived on the land, travelling and camping. Okalik participated in traditional caribou hunts.

When he was five years old, Okalik went to elementary school in Pangnirtung. School was a challenge for Okalik. Classes were taught in English, a language he did not speak or understand. He was then sent to a residential school in Iqaluit.

Okalik's teen years were difficult. He struggled with the law, serving a short prison sentence for breaking and entering. When Okalik was 14 years old, his older brother committed suicide after spending time in jail for a minor crime. The death affected Okalik deeply, and it helped inspire him to become a lawyer.

BORN Paul Okalik was born on May 26, 1964, in Pangnirtung, Nunavut, to Auyaluk and Annie Okalik.

FAMILY Okalik is the father of three children, Shasta, Jordan, and Beatrice. He also has a granddaughter, Brynn.

EDUCATION Okalik earned a bachelor of arts degree and a bachelor of laws degree.

CAREER Okalik has worked as a lawyer, a member of the Legislative Assembly of Nunavut, and as the territory's first premier. He is also a public speaker.

"[W]e continue to press on for recognition of Inuit rights, especially in the areas of education and health care."

Developing Skills

Okalik's life changed in 1985. He was offered a research job with the Tungavik Federation of Nunavut. Okalik worked negotiating Inuit land claims with the government of Canada. In fact, he helped settle the 1993 Inuit land claim that led to the formation of Nunavut. Okalik is also

Queen Elizabeth visited Canada in 2002 to mark her Golden Jubilee, or 50th anniversary as queen. She met with Okalik in Iqaluit, Nunavut, the first stop on her tour.

known for supporting the rights of Inuit and other Aboriginal Peoples in Canada and around the world. He helped to create the Inuit Heritage Trust, which works to preserve Inuit culture and traditions, and the Nunavut Wildlife Management Board.

Okalik's success gave him the confidence to continue his education. It also helped increase his interest in politics. Okalik returned to school in his late 20s. After earning a degree from Carleton University in Ottawa, Ontario, he went to law school at the University of Ottawa. While working on his law degree, Okalik made the decision to enter politics. He felt it would help to make positive changes for his people. Okalik received his law degree in 1997.

The Path to Success

Three days before the 1999 election, Okalik's dream of being the first Inuk lawyer in the Northwest Territories and Nunavut came true. After working at a law firm to gain experience, he was called to the bar, which meant that he had officially become able to practise law. Less than three weeks later, the members of the assembly chose him as Nunavut's first premier.

Supporting Inuit values and traditions while building a new government for Nunavut was difficult. The Nunavut government had many issues it needed to address immediately. Premier Okalik focussed on reducing unemployment, improving housing shortages, constructing new schools, and increasing graduation rates. He also supported an education act that created new Inuit language and culture programs. In 2004, Okalik was re-elected to the Legislative Assembly and again was selected premier.

In 2008, Okalik was replaced as premier by Eva Aariak. He ran in the 2011 federal election from the riding of Nunavut to serve in the House of Commons but lost. He continues to be active in politics. Okalik also works internationally as a public speaker.

Accomplishments

1995 Okalik earns a bachelor of arts degree in political science from Carleton University.

1997 Okalik earns a bachelor of laws degree from the University of Ottawa.

1999 Okalik is elected to the Legislative Assembly of Nunavut and is chosen as the new territory's first premier.

2005 Carleton University gives Okalik an honorary doctor of laws degree.

2009 Okalik wins an achievement award for politics from the National Aboriginal Achievement Foundation, now called Indspire.

2010 The Legislative Assembly of Nunavut selects Okalik as its speaker.

Chief and Activist

Shawn A-in-chut Atleo

Canada has more than 630 First Nations communities. The Assembly of First Nations (AFN) is a national political organization that represents these communities. It was founded in 1967 as the National Indian Brotherhood. AFN members meet every year to decide its policies and goals. Most of the group's funding comes from the Department of Indian Affairs, which is part of the federal government.

Aboriginal activist Shawn A-in-chut Atleo is the national chief of the Assembly of First Nations. He also served as the AFN regional chief for British Columbia. For many years, there had been disagreements among

Atleo's Aboriginal heritage is very important to him. He has been influenced by ancient teachings, including *Hish-ook-ish Tsa'walk*, meaning "everything, everyone is connected," and *Hopiitalth*, which means "be helpful, caring to each other."

Personal Profile

the different Aboriginal chiefs in the province. Atleo ended the conflict by helping the chiefs create and approve a historic agreement of general goals called the Leadership Accord in 2005.

Atleo is also a hereditary chief of the Ahousaht First Nation in British Columbia. Atleo's traditional name, *A-in-chut*, means "everyone depends on you" in his native language. Although his name is an honour, it was also a large responsibility. Atleo believes that being raised in traditional Ahousaht ways has helped him in his work as a leader and politician.

Early Years

Shawn A-in-chut Atleo, born in 1967, was raised in Ahousaht. Ahousaht is a small Aboriginal community on Flores Island off the west coast of Vancouver Island, British Columbia. Residents and visitors can reach the island only by boat or seaplane.

As a child, Atleo spent a great deal of time with his grandparents. Atleo's parents were also an important influence. His mother and father are both teachers with doctorate degrees.

"Now, as we continue to walk in the steps set by our ancestors, we must have our eyes firmly focussed on our future."

Atleo always knew he would become a hereditary chief of his community. The Ahousaht First Nation traditionally trains its hereditary chiefs from a very young age. Atleo was raised to understand and respect the traditional ways used to make decisions and govern.

Ahousaht is a remote First Nations community. The word can be translated to mean "people living with their backs to the land and mountains on a beach along the open sea."

BORN Shawn A-in-chut Atleo was born on January 16, 1967, in Ahousaht on Flores Island, British Columbia. His parents, Richard and Marlene Renate Atleo, are both educators.

FAMILY Atleo and his wife, Nancy, have two grown children, Tyson and Tara.

EDUCATION Atleo holds a master of education degree from the University of Technology in Sydney, Australia.

CAREER Atleo is a hereditary chief. Other positions include a regional chief of the Assembly of First Nations, as well as its national chief.

“It’s our time. It’s our time to implement our treaties, to fulfil our rights and responsibilities; we are part of a global indigenous movement to resume our rightful place in the economy and stewardship of Mother Earth. It is our time to act on our future.”

Developing Skills

As a young boy, Atleo played soccer often with his father. He became a skilled player and dreamed of playing professionally. During college, he even got the chance to play in a semi-professional league.

For a time, Atleo thought of being a chef and ran a coffee shop. He chose to move into politics, however. He wanted to help Aboriginal Peoples in Canada improve their quality of life. In 2003, Atleo earned a master of education degree from the University of Technology in Sydney, Australia. The degree was designed for students interested in international development work, health and environmental issues, and the promotion of social fairness. The coursework is entirely online, so Atleo was able to complete his studies from his home on Flores Island. That same year, Atleo became the regional chief for the Assembly of First Nations in British Columbia.

Atleo was one of the first people in his family not to attend a residential school. During his career, he has made educating Canada’s young Aboriginals a priority. In 2008, Vancouver Island University named Atleo its chancellor because of his commitment to education. He became the first university chancellor of Aboriginal

Atleo was first elected as national chief of the Assembly of First Nations in 2009. In 2012, he was re-elected for a second term, earning 341 out of 512 votes from First Nations leaders across Canada.

heritage in British Columbia's history. In 2009, Atleo decided to run for the position of national chief of the Assembly of First Nations.

The Path to Success

The 2009 race to lead the Assembly of First Nations was close. Winning required the support of at least 60 percent of the First Nation chiefs. Although he was considered a front-runner, Atleo needed eight rounds of voting to win.

Atleo was only 42 years old when he took office as the leader of Canada's First Nations. He continues to share his message of respect for others with the people of Canada. His dream is to live in a country where everyone understands and respects one another.

Atleo also plays an international role as an Aboriginal leader. He led a group of people to help rebuild native communities in Indonesia damaged in 2004 by a huge tsunami, or sea wave. Atleo also participated in talks for the 2007 United Nations Declaration on the Rights of Indigenous Peoples. The declaration was adopted by the government of Canada in 2010.

Accomplishments

1999 Atleo is named the hereditary chief of the Ahousaht First Nation.

2003 After earning a master of education degree, Atleo becomes the regional chief for the Assembly of First Nations in British Columbia.

2008 Vancouver Island University names Atleo its chancellor.

2009 Atleo becomes the national chief of the Assembly of First Nations.

2010 Nipissing University in North Bay, Ontario, awards Atleo an honorary doctorate of laws. He is also named a councillor on the World Future Council, which addresses climate and energy issues.

2012 Atleo is re-elected as the national chief of the Assembly of First Nations to serve a second three-year term.

Politician and Cabinet Member

Leona Aglukkaq

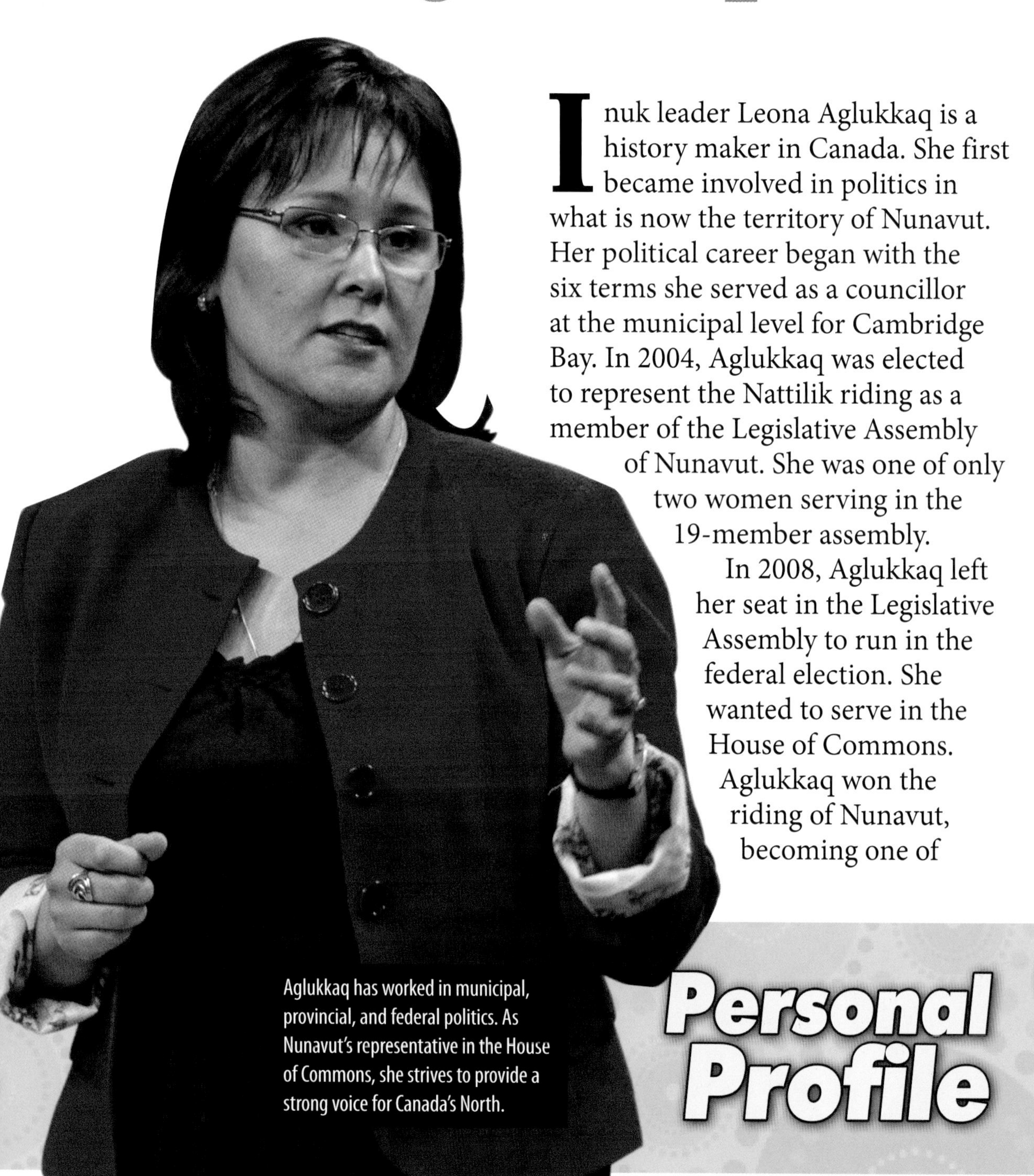

Aglukkaq has worked in municipal, provincial, and federal politics. As Nunavut's representative in the House of Commons, she strives to provide a strong voice for Canada's North.

Inuk leader Leona Aglukkaq is a history maker in Canada. She first became involved in politics in what is now the territory of Nunavut. Her political career began with the six terms she served as a councillor at the municipal level for Cambridge Bay. In 2004, Aglukkaq was elected to represent the Nattilik riding as a member of the Legislative Assembly of Nunavut. She was one of only two women serving in the 19-member assembly.

In 2008, Aglukkaq left her seat in the Legislative Assembly to run in the federal election. She wanted to serve in the House of Commons. Aglukkaq won the riding of Nunavut, becoming one of the first Inuk women elected to Parliament. As a new MP, Aglukkaq was given the very important position of minister of Health, responsible for maintaining and improving the health of all Canadians. Leona Aglukkaq made history when she became the first Inuk to serve in the federal Cabinet.

Early Years

Leona Aglukkaq was born in 1967. She grew up in Thom Bay, Taloyoak, and Gjoa Haven, which were then in the Northwest Territories but are now within Nunavut. Her father was a hunter. Her mother, Miriam Aglukkaq, is a teacher in Gjoa Haven. Aglukkaq grew up speaking Inuktitut. She learned English when she started school.

Aglukkaq left home to attend secondary school in Yellowknife, in the Northwest Territories. After completing her studies, she returned home. Aglukkaq first became interested in pursuing a career in politics when she was 14 years old. She saw a need for leadership in her community. Aglukkaq believed she had the determination to make positive changes.

"We believe that youth are the cornerstone of our communities. As such, one of our goals is to ensure our children enjoy a safer, healthier, and more prosperous future."

As the current minister of Health, Aglukkaq has tackled a variety of health issues facing Canadians, including diabetes, HIV, drug safety, and mental health.

BORN Leona Aglukkaq was born on June 28, 1967, in Inuvik, Northwest Territories, now Nunavut.

FAMILY Aglukkaq is married to Robert MacNeil. They have a son, Cooper.

EDUCATION Aglukkaq studied management at Arctic College in Iqaluit.

CAREER Aglukkaq served as a councillor in municipal government and in the Legislative Assembly of Nunavut.

Developing Skills

Aglukkaq was always a hardworking, determined student. She chose to study management at Arctic College in Iqaluit. While she was there, she set a goal for herself. She wanted to be a deputy minister before reaching the age of 30.

Aglukkaq achieved her goal when she began working for the governments of the Northwest Territories and then Nunavut, after that new territory was created in 1999. She served as the deputy clerk of the Legislative Assembly of Nunavut. She also worked as the deputy minister for Culture, Language, Elders, and Youth. She decided to run for elected office in 2004.

The Path to Success

After winning her seat in the Legislative Assembly of Nunavut in 2004, Aglukkaq was given various responsibilities. She was chosen by other members of the legislature to serve on the executive council as finance minister and **house leader**.

Following the 2011 federal election, Aglukkaq was sworn in as the minister of Health, retaining the role she has held since 2008.

"As mothers, fathers, sisters, brothers, cousins, and friends, we can all reflect upon the great impact women have had in shaping our Canada and making a difference in our world."

Later, she became the minister of Health and Social Services and the minister responsible for the Status of Women.

At this time, Nunavut was still establishing itself as a new territory. Its people faced many social and health challenges. There was a shortage of medical staff and a lack of funding for health care. Many people in Nunavut had to travel to other provinces for medical treatment. As minister of Health, Aglukkaq worked to open new facilities in communities such as Rankin Inlet and Cambridge Bay, allowing patients to receive treatment closer to home.

Throughout her career in politics, Aglukkaq has been dedicated to the health and well-being of all Canadians. Her first term in Parliament brought several challenges, including the 2009 H1N1 virus or "swine flu" outbreak that threatened to spread around the world. Aglukkaq was widely praised for her calm management of the crisis in Canada. Her leadership helped Aglukkaq win re-election in 2011.

Aglukkaq was also appointed minister of the Canadian Northern Economic Development Agency (CanNor) in 2011. CanNor is focussed on providing services that support economic development in Nunavut, the Northwest Territories, and Yukon. This appointment helps Leona Aglukkaq to continue showing a commitment to her homeland.

Accomplishments

2004 Aglukkaq is elected to the Legislative Assembly of Nunavut for the Nattilik riding and serves until 2008.

2008 Aglukkaq becomes the member of Parliament for Nunavut and is appointed minister of Health.

2009 Equal Voice, a not-for-profit organization that supports women in Canadian politics, gives Aglukkaq an EVE Award for her achievements.

2011 Aglukkaq is re-elected to the House of Commons and reappointed as health minister. She earns nearly half of the vote, defeating former Nunavut premier Paul Okalik. She is also appointed minister of the Canadian Northern Economic Development Agency.

2012 Aglukkaq wins an achievement award for politics from Indspire.

Write a Biography

All of the parts of a biography work together to tell the story of a person's life. Find out how these elements combine by writing a biography. Begin by choosing a person whose story fascinates you. You will have to research the person's life by using library books and reliable websites. You can also email the person or write him or her a letter. The person might agree to answer your questions directly.

Use a concept web, such as the one below, to guide you in writing the biography. Answer each of the questions listed using the information you have gathered. Each heading on the concept web will form an important part of the person's story.

Parts of a Biography

Early Life

Where and when was the person born?

What is known about the person's family and friends?

Did the person grow up in unusual circumstances?

Growing Up

Who had the most influence on the person?

Did he or she receive assistance from others?

Did the person have a positive attitude?

Developing Skills

What was the person's education?

What was the person's first job or work experience?

What obstacles did the person overcome?

Early Achievements

What was the person's most important early success?

What processes does this person use in his or her work?

Which of the person's traits were most helpful in his or her work?

Person Today

Has the person received awards or recognition for accomplishments?

What is the person's life's work?

How have the person's accomplishments served others?

Internet Resources

Aboriginal Affairs and Northern Development
Run by the government of Canada, this regularly updated site features hundreds of links related to political, cultural, and legal issues of interest to Aboriginal Peoples.

WEBSITE: www.aadnc-aandc.gc.ca/eng/1100100010002

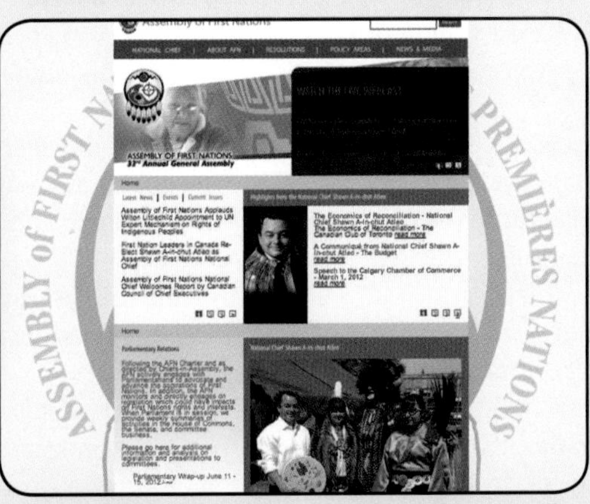

Assembly of First Nations
The website features news, events, and issues related to Aboriginal Canadians.

WEBSITE: www.afn.ca/index.php/en

Native Leaders of Canada
This site has short biographies of Canada's great historical and contemporary Aboriginal leaders and politicians.

WEBSITE: www.newfederation.org/Native_Leaders/Index.htm

Glossary

Aboriginal: a term that refers to the First Nations, Métis, and Inuit peoples of Canada

accord: an official agreement

advocate: a person who supports a cause

ancestors: family members who lived in the past

Cabinet: a group of members of a legislature selected by the prime minister or premier to head government departments and to develop policies and plans

Constitution: a system of laws by which a government is organized

democracy: a type of government in which the people elect representatives to pass laws and make decisions for them

federal: of or relating to the national government

house leader: the member of a legislative body who is chosen to represent a political party in that body

House of Commons: the lower house of Parliament; its members are elected by Canadian citizens

indigenous peoples: groups of people native to an area

Inuk: a person who is a member of the Inuit

Legislative Assembly: a lawmaking body that governs a province or territory

members of Parliament (MPs): people elected to the House of Commons; Canada's Parliament is a lawmaking body composed of the House of Commons, the Senate, and the monarchy

Métis: a person who is of mixed Aboriginal and European descent

minister: the head of a government department

political party: a group of people with the same beliefs about what government should do

premier: the chief minister of the government of a province or a territory

prime minister: the head of the federal government in Canada

reserve: land set aside by the federal government for the use and occupancy of a First Nations group

residential school: a government-run school for Aboriginal students that taught European-Canadian ways of life and forbade the use of Aboriginal languages

riding: an election district

Index